AUSTRALIA

Written by
Rebecca Phillips-Bartlett

Gareth Stevens
PUBLISHING

TRAVEL THE WORLD!

Please visit our website, www.garethstevens.com. For a free color catalog of all our high-quality books, call toll free 1-800-542-2595 or fax 1-877-542-2596.

Cataloging-in-Publication Data

Names: Phillips-Bartlett, Rebecca.
Title: Australia / Rebecca Phillips-Bartlett.
Description: New York : Gareth Stevens Publishing, 2024. | Series: Travel the world! | Includes glossary and index.
Identifiers: ISBN 9781538288276 (pbk.) | ISBN 9781538288283 (library bound) | ISBN 9781538288290 (ebook)
Subjects: LCSH: Australia--Juvenile literature. | Australia--Description and travel--Juvenile literature.
Classification: LCC DU96.P455 2024 | DDC 994--dc23

Published in 2024 by
Gareth Stevens Publishing
2544 Clinton St.
Buffalo, NY 14224

Written by: Rebecca Phillips-Bartlett
Edited by: Elise Carraway
Designed by: Amy Li & Isabella Croker

Photo Credits

All images are courtesy of Shutterstock.com, unless otherwise specified. With thanks to Getty Images, Thinkstock Photo and iStockphoto. Recurring images – ONYXprj, Ihor Biliavskyi, EMJAY SMITH, Olleg, alexmstudio. Cover images – Wouter Tolenaars, EMJAY SMITH, grop, Slowga, Jemastock, Sky and glass, curiosity, N.Style, Olleg.. 2–3 – Petr Kratochvila. 4–5 – KittyVector, N.Style, Nadzin, Net Vector, Olga1818, Sino Studio. 6–7 – AnnstasAg, crbellette, EcoPrint, eo Tang, Modvector. 8–9 – alokojha, Andrea Izzotti, mcography, Midorie, moremari, Nadya_Art, Rasith Wijesuriya. 10–11 – Andrea Izzotti, David Dennis, klyaksun, Mariangela Cruz, trabantos, VVadyab Pico. 12–13 – Amanita Silvicora, Andrii Slonchak, Arjuna Gihan, Avant Visual, Lawrence_Chung, Steve Lovegrove. 14–15 – ONYXprj, Sky and glass, GraphicsRF.com, FiledIMAGE, Ankit M, gg-foto, Divektorin Studio. 16–17 – inavanhateren, Aleksandar Todorovic, jejim, Jodie Johnson, curiosity. 18–19 – Chris Howey, Andreas Hahn, biplane_desire, Hans Wagemaker, mehmetaligrafik, marcobrivio.photo. 20–21 – Paul Burdett, Edward Haylan, V_E, ShustrikS, Martin Valigursky, Zaie, meritpro. 22–23 – inithings, Stanislav Novoselov, Mari Dambi.

© 2023 Booklife Publishing
This edition is published by arrangement with Booklife Publishing

All rights reserved. No part of this book may be reproduced in any form without permission in writing from the publisher, except by a reviewer.

Printed in the United States of America

CPSIA compliance information: Batch #CSGS24: For further information contact Gareth Stevens at 1-800-542-2595.

Find us on

CONTENTS

PAGE 4	We Are Going on a Trip
PAGE 6	Kakadu National Park
PAGE 7	Uluru
PAGE 8	Shark Bay
PAGE 9	Namburg National Park
PAGE 10	Adelaide Botanic Garden
PAGE 11	Kangaroo Island
PAGE 12	Tasmania
PAGE 13	Hasting Caves
PAGE 14	Great Ocean Road
PAGE 15	Melbourne Cricket Ground
PAGE 16	Canberra
PAGE 17	Bondi Beach
PAGE 18	Sydney Opera House
PAGE 19	Sydney Harbour Beach
PAGE 20	Wheel of Brisbane
PAGE 21	The Great Barrier Reef
PAGE 22	Home
PAGE 24	Glossary and Index

WORDS THAT LOOK LIKE <u>THIS</u> CAN BE FOUND IN THE GLOSSARY ON PAGE 24.

WE ARE GOING ON A TRIP

Hi, I am Elijah. My family and I are going on a road trip in Australia. I have never been to Australia before, so I am really excited to see lots of new things.

Mom, Dad, and me.

KAKADU NATIONAL PARK

Our first stop is Kakadu <u>National Park</u>. Kakadu is Australia's largest national park. There is lots of very old art on the rocks at Kakadu. The art shows how people at Kakadu used to live.

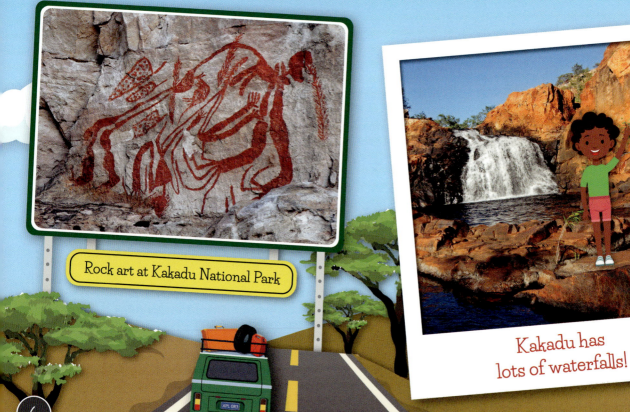

Rock art at Kakadu National Park

Kakadu has lots of waterfalls!

ULURU

Uluru is one of the most famous <u>landmarks</u> in Australia. It is about 500 million years old. That is about twice as old as the dinosaurs! Uluru is almost 1,150 feet (350 m) high.

Uluru looks like it is a different color at different times of day.

It is brown during the day...

This way: Uluru

...but looks orange or red at sunset!

SHARK BAY

We go to lots of beaches in Shark Bay! At Monkey Mia beach we see bottlenose dolphins. My favorite beach is Shell Beach. Shell Beach is made of seashells instead of sand!

SHELL BEACH

DOLPHIN AT MONKEY MIA BEACH

This way: Shark Bay

NAMBURG NATIONAL PARK

The best thing about Namburg National Park is the Pinnacles Desert. The Pinnacles are <u>natural</u> <u>sculptures</u>. They are made of a rock called limestone, which comes from broken-down seashells and <u>coral</u>.

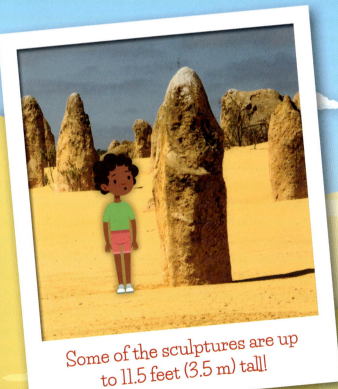

Some of the sculptures are up to 11.5 feet (3.5 m) tall!

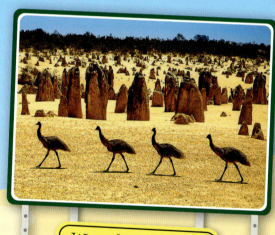

We see lots of animals, such as emus.

ADELAIDE BOTANIC GARDEN

In Adelaide, we go to the Botanic Garden. There are lots of beautiful plants. There is even a museum where I learn how people can use plants for things such as food and healing people.

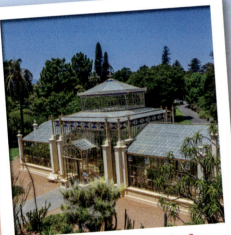

A glass building called the Palm House

The Botanic Garden is very pretty!

KANGAROO ISLAND

We take a boat to Kangaroo Island. From the boat we can see lots of seals and sea lions. It is even better when we get to the island. We see real koalas and kangaroos!

A GROUP OF KANGAROOS

A wild koala

TASMANIA

We also go to another island called Tasmania. We visit Bridestowe Lavender Estate and eat lavender-flavored ice cream. Beyond the lavender field, there is a view of Mount Arthur.

The lavender is bright purple!

Now entering: Tasmania

We see a Tasmanian devil. You can only find them in Tasmania.

12

HASTING CAVES

The caves are deep so there are lots of stairs.

We go on a tour of the Hasting Caves. Inside the caves there are lots of stalactites. Stalactites are rocks that hang down from the roof of the cave.

The cave's roof is covered in stalactites.

GREAT OCEAN ROAD

We drive along the Great Ocean Road. It is very pretty. The most interesting thing we see is the Twelve Apostles. They are rocks that used to be joined to the <u>cliffs</u>, but now they are separate.

Great Ocean Road

They are called the Twelve Apostles, but some of them have fallen apart over time.

MELBOURNE CRICKET GROUND

MELBOURNE CRICKET GROUND FROM THE SKY

Inside the cricket stadium

Australia's national sport is cricket. This means that cricket is a very important sport for Australia. In Melbourne, we visit one of the world's largest cricket stadiums called Melbourne Cricket Ground.

CANBERRA

Canberra is the capital city of Australia. Even though the city is quite new, it is full of places to learn about Australia's history and culture. We visit the National Museum of Australia.

The National Museum of Australia

The outside of the museum is very colorful!

Now entering: Canberra

BONDI BEACH

Bondi Beach is Australia's most famous beach. The golden sand is perfect for building sandcastles! From some parts of the beach, we can see whales!

There are lots of people surfing in the ocean.

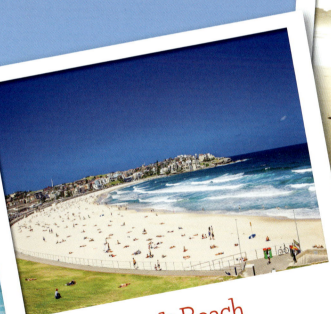

Bondi Beach

SYDNEY OPERA HOUSE

Even though it has opera in its name, you can see all sorts of shows at Sydney Opera House. It was only meant to take four years to build, but it took 14 years!

Sydney Opera House is one of Australia's most famous landmarks.

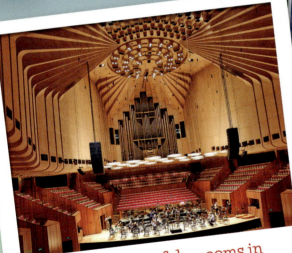

This is one of the rooms in Sydney Opera House.

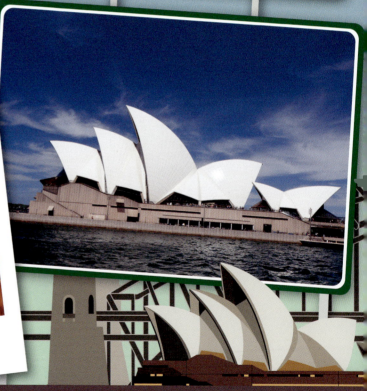

SYDNEY HARBOUR BRIDGE

We climb Sydney Harbour Bridge! The bridge is huge, so it takes over a thousand steps to reach the top. Sydney Harbour Bridge is often known as "the Coat Hanger" because of its shape.

Sydney Harbour Bridge

This is me climbing Sydney Harbour Bridge!

WHEEL OF BRISBANE

THE WHEEL OF BRISBANE IS 197 FEET (60 M) TALL!

We do not spend very long in Brisbane, so we go on the Wheel of Brisbane to see lots of other landmarks. I see Brisbane's Botanical Garden, the Goodwill Bridge, and Mount Coot-tha.

At night, the Wheel is lit up with bright colors.

THE GREAT BARRIER REEF

The Great Barrier Reef is one of the <u>Seven Natural Wonders of the World</u>. It is millions of years old and home to lots of different types of animals. It is made up of coral.

THIS IS WHAT THE GREAT BARRIER REEF LOOKS LIKE FROM THE SKY.

Healthy coral is bright and colorful!

HOME

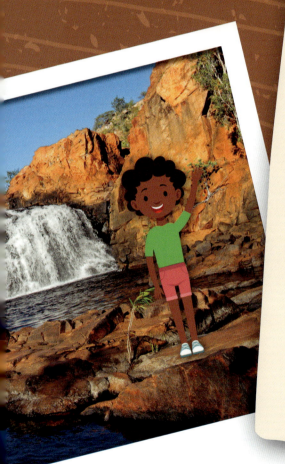

I had such a great time in Australia! I loved finding out about the interesting animals and history. There was so much to learn.

I would love to go to Australia again. I want to go to the National Library of Australia and to the Perisher Ski Resort!

See you soon!

Love, Elijah x

GLOSSARY

CAVES	large openings underground in rocks and hills
CLIFFS	the high, steep sides of mountains or land
CORAL	small animals that live on rocks in warm seas and make hard, colorful outer skeletons. They group together to make coral reefs.
CULTURE	the traditions, ideas, and ways of life of a group of people
LANDMARKS	places or buildings that are easily recognized
NATIONAL PARK	a protected site with lots of nature
NATURAL	found in nature and not made by people
SCULPTURES	objects, such as statues, made through carving or molding
SEVEN NATURAL WONDERS OF THE WORLD	seven places that are especially known for their beauty and not built by people

INDEX

animals 9, 21–22
art 6
beaches 5, 8, 17
capital cities 16
caves 5, 13
corals 9, 21
history 16, 22
kangaroos 5, 11
landmarks 7, 18, 20
lavender 12
plants 10
sports 15
waterfalls 6